Brian R. Martens' poetry book *Merlin's Wing* resonates with yearning, humor, and intelligence. But mostly it is about passion. From the remolding of a candle that held "intimate conversations," to a child's cooing that becomes a dialog, to "bending thoughts into fudge brownies of longing," his exploration of feelings reaches into our own life.

This is accessible poetry asking questions like, "What can turn a life?" or "which light are you drawn to?" A love poem says, "You have waited a year for this swoon." A walk in the woods asks us to "trust trees more than newscasts." A hand accidentally rests on a stranger's arm in a museum, and we are imagining what loss feels like. We are in Paris, in Sri Lanka, walking in the woods, picking buckeye blossoms, loving a grandchild, all with a deep connection and yearning for life.

Brian asks about himself, "Is poetry enough to heal my own mind?" I think this book will go a long way to answer that question.

—Linda Loveland Reid, author of *Touch of Magenta* and *Something in Stone*

Brian R. Martens' *Merlin's Wing* takes readers on a poetic journey into the sacred interplay between myth, childhood, and self-actualization. With vivid imagery and a profound sense of wonder, Martens reconnects us to the intuitive mind, the sacred gift so often lost in a world of rationality.

Through tender moments like those in "California Buckeye" and "The Quiet Home," Martens captures the magic of youth and the enduring myths that shape us. Whether evoking the Bushmen's survival in "Bushmen" or the soaring presence of a raven in *Merlin's Wing,* his poetry invites us to see life with the eyes of a child—curious, trusting, and open to mystery.

Merlin's Wing is more than a collection of poems; it's an invitation to rediscover the myths in our own lives, to dream deeply, and to embrace the unseen. Martens' words hum with the timeless joy of exploration, urging us all to grow our wings and embark on boundless journeys.

—Poet Ed Coletti is the author of *Apollo Blue's Harp* (2019), *When Hearts Outlive Minds* (2011), and *The Problem With Breathing* (2015).

Merlin's Wing

New and Selected Poems:
2005 to 2022 by Brian R. Martens

Luchador Press
Big Tuna, Texas

Copyright © Brian R. Martens, 2025
First Edition: 1 3 5 7 9 10 8 6 4 2
ISBN:979-8-89975-002-1
LCCN: 2025938306

Cover art © by Caren D. Catterall, printmaker,
  carencatterall.com
Title page and interior images: Michael Hofmann

Acknowledgments:

I am grateful for the support and assistance I receive for my writing. Teachers, mentors, and friends have been invaluable in learning about poetry and accumulating life skills which go into writing a good poem. All the poets I witness at open mics are part of my poetic voice:

Margo Perin and Meg Hamill with CA Poets in the Schools have mentored and supported my efforts to teach poetry in the schools. Local poets and "Open Mics" are consistent supporters as well as a thriving poetic community.

Diane Frank and Terry Lucas have added depth and consistency to my showing up for poetry. The positive feedback has been supportive and has stretched my concepts of what poetry is about, and nourished the deep well of emotion that nourishes all poetry. Special gratitude goes to Terry Lucas. His editing, conversations, and grounded advice keeps my poetic voice alive and current.

I want to give special gratitude to Marvin Hiemstra, who passed away in 2024 from a fall. We first met at the poetry open mic at Aquas Café in Petaluma. He introduced himself afterwards and he liked my poetry.

We became friends. He shared his home and life with me in San Francisco and we shared poetry at other events. He grew up in Iowa near my hometown of Martensdale. The colleges we went to were in the same conference. Marvin was always encouraging and went out of his way to travel across the country to share his poetry. Blessings to you Marvin on your next path.

Blessings to Angeles Arrien Ph.D. for teaching me Haiku and opening Indigenous cultures for me. Your mentorship is a guiding light. Waights Taylor published my first book and promoted my poetry to other authors and poets.

Gratitude to Marguerite Wildenhain and Dean Schwarz who started my first creative life with pottery by teaching me the rugged steps to see inside nature and my creative spirit.

Love and full hugs to Trevor and Natalie, our threesome navigated growing up and learning how to be a family, my biggest supporters.

Linda Loveland Reid is a sparkling reminder and mentor showing how creativity can bring community together; she must have fairies working for her around the clock.

Our lives are not solo excursions. I am affected and supported by the seen and unseen. The wind, water, earth and light are part of me and inform my every step. What would I do without Nature? Remembering is a factor of poetry: immersing, delving, guiding, exploring all the words that have lead me to this place and time. Remember the good words.

I want to thank all the poets and ancestors who have spoken before us. Their shoulders are broad and strong allowing current and future writers to stand strong, open, and fearless in their writing.

TABLE OF CONTENTS

1. Turn a Life

2. First Kiss

3. Moon and White Buffalo

4. Bushmen

1

Turn a Life

"The intuitive mind is a sacred gift and the rational mind is a faithful servant. We have created a society that honors the servant and has forgotten the gift."
-Albert Einstein

Merlin's Wing—Raven

Iridescent black, glowing colors
speaking the wisdom of myth,
your cawing musical voice
showing the illusive trickster.

Your trick, playing me,
I gasp as you dive,
speeding like a tucked bullet,
vision carving sky and nest,
wings touch the sound of air.

Sculpting myth to trust the unseen.
Legend follows you as I grow my wings.
Tell me more stories,
dip your wings into gold.

You perch on my shoulder
speaking your language to my hollow ear.
Your antics of flight follow.
I feel you rise, wings
bursting through fog, light, and air.

Turn a Life

> "And the man in the black coat turns, and goes back down
> the hill, no one knows why he came or why he turned
> away and did not climb the hill."
>> -Robert Bly

> "Turn sideways into the light...and disappear..."
>> -David Whyte

What can turn a life?
To which light are you drawn,
light the moth prefers at night,
light of noon sun,
moon's full light,
light within
your heart burning with desire?

Which light has caught your attention,
caused you to look sideways,
where you saw a glimpse,
a gleaming image you had not seen before?

What soul-same vision did you discover,
caused you to look again,
questioned a new horizon, up the hill,
pivoting to turn a life?

The Voice

The child's voice drowned,
sinking to the bottom of the well,
together with glimmering coins of promise,
hidden in darkness.

I am here now, bubbles of breath
breaking the surface of calm.
The impending horizon,
here, the voice down here,
languishing, longing to be heard.

The sound of one diminished voice
faintly recognized as my own, waiting
in the well of wishes, wanting nothing
but listening.

I drop the slow rope into the well, bubbles
escaping. It slackens—bottom.
My eyes water as connection is made, something
has dawned, attached—tears, sadness, torment
awakened in this now turbulent water.

I tug—
the well full of expectations.
My hands will not stop pulling,
the body must know.

My practice is pulling weight.
Bringing up the drowned voice, my head
numb with fear, forgetting. My arms
continue to carry the burden of knowing.
My practice is pulling weight.

As the water clears, I see a young boy,
eyes aglow with recognition, bubbles
of his breath breaking surface, calling.
His tiny hands full of coins.
He is breathing—he's breathing.

I lift him out of the water,
to the edge of the well,
water pouring off his body,
as words gush out of his shivering lips.
I set him, grounded,
next to the well,
I listen—I listen,
and I listen.

Getting Out of the Way

Poetry is a locomotive, blaring,
blasting, incapable of being stopped.
Poetry is a timid child,
waiting patiently with sight of a sage
perplexed at my paltry perfection.

I marvel at the balance of poetry,
when to step out of the way,
when to take a child by the hand
and listen to that voice, moving together.

This dance of poetry
a Cha-Cha, Swing, Two-Step, Tango
a satisfying Salsa or Fandango.

Words forming a line to be chosen,
to fit a rhythm, a cadence, music.
Crowding, pushing in place, colliding,
anticipating, finding the final stop.

Silence beckons with a
faith in words, without missing a beat.
Surprised steps become seen,
visualized into a path.

Poetry, a locomotion of agitated words
moving, inviting, blending into a search
for the back step of human creation.

The Girl with a Pink Balloon

She ducked—a bold move—
under my leg, propped on a
shopping cart, a tunnel to explore,
her pink balloon rising after.

I watched her go, liberation in a pale
sleeveless dress and pink balloon.
She never looked back
to see the effect of her exploration.

The task won. Her spirit aflame
with purpose, she marched
uncaring, daring, like her helium balloon,
into rarified air,
a life born to rise.

The Held Mistake

My father is fixing the bailer
with his dad and a watching farmer.

The gravity of critical, embedded
in his right shoulder,
visceral verdict in his right ear
entering through his right side,
unprotected, willing to take
the blow of fault and failure.

Arrow of blame sent
from his dad and the farmer.
They're justified, passing the
thread of ancestral shadow.
The pride of being
right cloaked to preserve
the impeccable self.

This moment holds a lifetime.
Wound hidden
deep, partially let go to
attach to my right shoulder,
preserving the shadow,
alert for the next wound.

He tells his story to finally let go,
allowing me to learn about fathers,
the wounding, and to ease the pain
in my right side, his right side,
shoulder, and ear—to trust again.

He tells his story to say what is so,
to speak what the body needs,
allowing a full breath to enter and exit
my full, open, clear, strong heart.

Candle

A failed wick, lost in wax,
pieces of match and dirt.
Finding a new wick,
I melt the old candle, save the old wax
because it holds candle-lit dinners,
Thanksgiving smell,
late night movies with buttered popcorn.

The wax held aromas of grandkids
stalking around the house,
intimate conversations,
Motown on the radio, and
a rose whiff of gratitude.

The old candle had to be reformed
into a new image.
I added the scent of frankincense,
myrrh, the scent of a fresh baby,
newly born. I added cinnamon
and a dash of togetherness
to bind all the disparate parts.

Poured the hot wax into new glass,
dropped the wick, anchored
to the bottom. The candle sat to harden,
anticipating new light.

In the evening, a sound
of fresh rain on roof, I ignited
match to candle, the wick
took the hungry flame,
popped, sputtered wax,
formed a solid light.

At once, the room filled
with a savory scent, new ideas,
conversations blossomed.
This flame, this fire,
a promethean gift,
here again to give light
to a new beginning.

That Day at the Museum

My wife and I went to the de Young Museum.
We decided to separate and walked aimlessly.
I was staring at a painting that caught
my attention, when a woman's
hand wrapped around my forearm.

An unfamiliar voice said, "Dear,
isn't that painting lovely, it would
look marvelous in our hallway."
Both of our heads turned to each other,
she recoiled, and I said, "it would look
marvelous in our hallway."

She apologized for touching my arm.
I assured her no harm was done.
I watched as she walked away,
returned to her group and husband,
explained the shock of what happened.

I turned back to a painting,
feeling that I knew her—perhaps
her mysterious smile, or the smile
in the painting in the previous room.

I imagined lunch with her,
discussing art, the Renaissance.
Sitting at a window table in the museum
café, surrounded by people
and thoughts, like the rising aroma
from our cups of coffee.

I asked her if we could go home
and make love in front of the beautiful
painting we had just bought,
drink champagne and spill
kisses all over the floor.

Then, I felt a familiar hand weave into mine
and a voice say, "Honey, let's get lunch."

The Rilke

Homage for Rilke's poem, "The Panther"

Timid in hat and coat,
sitting on a bench
in the Paris Zoo,
he stares.

Sitting apart from comfort,
his body hidden,
barring him from an opening
to see into the animals.

He comes day after day
observing me, testing his will
to discover a path, to pierce
and expose inside.

Daily, imprisoned within hat and coat,
his vision paces less, moves further,
until he trusts.

Through time, his introspection
sees past his contentment,
begins to penetrate
inside my animal essence.

His eyes seize me,
without the believed bars
passing, knows the thread is felt
between us, and suddenly he's aware

I am Panther.

Why I Trust Poets

They have webbing between their toes,
see in darkened spaces,
have a small nest in their hair.

One fingernail is a small claw,
they have a tuft of fur behind one ear.

The poet has lived disguised,
nurtured in a shroud of words
and cracks of light.

Their speech transcending
any spoken language.

The Poet knows the craft of truth
and falsehood, can distinguish
between flowers and faith,
knows the voice as a spoken symbol.

The poet apprentices
the natural world,
bridging differences
into an ecstatic presence.

Devil and the Barber Chair–
First Memory

Sitting in a barber chair
waiting for a haircut,
the barber in the mirror
in front of me.

His face an evil devil, horns,
ugly, menacing, wielding an axe.

I awoke to the loud THUD
of the axe burying into my neck.
I sit up in bed afraid, scared, confused.
I hear the familiar voices of my folks
downstairs, talking with friends.

Still afraid, whimpering,
I go down the stairs
in the dark slits of light
flowing from beneath the door
at the bottom of the stairs.

Sitting on the bottom step,
listening to their conversation.
Laughing, joking,
my parents drinking with friends.

I knock quietly
to get their attention, ask for help,
comfort, to understand what's happening.

Mom helps me upstairs into bed.
She sees nightmare on my face
tucking me in, saying
I am safe.

I don't remember how long it took
to fall asleep.
The dream never returned,
but followed me
through my life, like seasons.

A first memory, now watery, mixed with forever.

Make prayers to the Raven.
Raven that is,
Raven that was,
Raven that always will be.
Make prayers to the Raven.
Raven, bring us luck.

-From the Koyukon people, *Ravensong*

"The Koyukon are the northwestern most tribe of the Athabaskan Indians, situated near the Koyukon and Yukon rivers. Their ancient stories constitute their oral tradition which exists from what they call "Distant Time.""

The central figure in this ancient world was the Raven who was its creator and who engineered many of its metamorphoses. Raven, the contradiction—omnipotent clown, benevolent mischief-maker, buffoon, and deity. It was he, transformed into a spruce needle, who was swallowed by a woman so she would give birth to him as a boy. When the boy was old enough to play, he took from beneath a blanket in her house the missing sun and rolled it to the door. Once outside, he became Raven again and flew up to return the sun to the sky, making the earth light again."

-excerpts and adaption by author, from
Richard K. Nelson's book *Make Prayers to the Raven*, pages16-17.

2

First Kiss

First Kiss

"August 2nd,"
"What year?"
"Who?"
I found written on a scrap of paper
in an old file.
I thought of throwing it away.

I gazed at the note, amazed.
I burned through anticipation and wonder
searching the seared aloneness
now stalking me.
The mosaic of moments
seeking transmutation.

Dreamy romantic music
has kept me here,
wallowing in an old affection.
I recycle this scrap of my life.

After a Child's Nap

I pull him from his crib,
into my arms, warm,
settling him there after a brief cry.

He holds court, administers
things that need saying,
none of which I understand.

He points to a window and begins.
I think he is describing a tree
across the street, in colors,
and judges the sky by its weight.

Artistically, he expounds,
with voice inflection and tone,
whimsical, melodious, infectious.

I don't understand, yet I believe.
I trust his awareness.
I don't want him to stop, ever.

He sounds like manna,
a voice from Eden, echoing,
Adam's voice or Eve's
or a blend of the first voices.

A voice soft yet knowing.
It all makes perfect sense to him,
as he continues, in a whisper,
his lips bursting with mysterious words.

His tone, awakened bells
splashed with rose water, a delicate love
song sung by lovers.

The language of angels bubbling
from his lips, more
gesturing, pointing.

An experience of art,
or Jesus speaking his foreign language
understanding there will be enough
fishes and loaves for everyone.

Cate

I saw your picture
in Poets & Writers magazine,
fell in love.

You, an accomplished poet
with red-hot lips,
short hair, slightly ruffled.
Your sure stance and gaze
embody your fearless poems.

A teacher of words, one
who can strangle a sentence
into submission, rendering words
into grit, flowers, faith.

I searched you and found you smoke,
have a boyfriend on the East Coast.
I read your fierce interview,
no room for doubt.

Crafting these words for you—
imagination
bending thought into fudge brownies
of longing.

Wanting a meeting of poetic dreams,
constructing a poem to share,
reflect, and for "us" to exist.

All this,
before I had a chance to say to you—
I like your poems.

Matilda and the Golden Finger

I was sitting in my Ozark Trail camping chair,
inches from the concrete floor,
resting from work with friends,
tearing down, preparing
for new construction.

A child of eighteen months approached me.
I met her parents briefly during the day,
trying to remember her name, surprised,
I listened and watched intently.

Leaning against my leg, she crawled
into my lap. Her parents and friends,
anxious about her vulnerability,
her mother wanting to protect her,
while I felt humbled by her play.

I lifted her, sat her against my chest,
as she looked out at friends, family, safe.
We sat, I listened to make her comfortable.
I wanted to feel like her teddy bear,
her favorite toy, a bottle of warm milk.

Looking at the ceiling, she pointed
with a finger of her tiny,
cupped hand. She began to speak and

describe with glowing resolve,
which I didn't understand.

Letting go of everything and everyone
in the room, I grasped her gushing.
Together, as one seamless body,
she spoke as she gestured
to the large, pointed skylight.

Her lips turned gold as they expressed
seeing Angels and cherubs floating
in the colorific hue of light
streaming from the sky. Genius poured
from her lips as her finger turned to gold.

Her voice, floating, luminous.
Her angelic face enlightened
with passion and knowledge
of how to pledge
her golden words
from filigreed finger.

Thanksgiving Eve

We met over a drink and soup.
The mood spicy, electric,
your breath in my ear,
wanting to be kissed with breathless passion.

Raven hair with velvet skin,
brushing my arm, feeling the way
to bridge the gap of age.
Both of our bodies saying yes.

Moving to the patio, we shared
the comfort of hands and face,
mouths touching and navigating
the warm waters of unexplored lips.
The tide sweeping away doubt and fear,
trusting the moment.

Your words led to confusion, retreat.
We talked navigating, finding a path
in the midst of collision, ideas, passion.

A brief burst of galvanic bodies.
Simmering magnetic looks embrace
our craving.

A special, magical surprise encounter.
A thanksgiving of trust.

Dreaming in Trees

I'm walking to the river,
with my grandson
asleep in his stroller.
The tiny wheels a rhythm
of crunching leaves,
rolling gravel, smooth dirt,
twigs crumbling.

This sleepy rhythm—
walking, strolling,
wind, birds, breath,
in, out through his fluid chest—
keeps his dream alive.

The fertile unconscious
hears the Earth speak,
a walking meditation
mesmerizing this Buddha.

Not to wake him
from his appointed dream,
merging this nature with his nature,
I sit to watch the nomadic river.

Standing up, I again embark,
calmness his pillow,
as he sleeps silently.

Strolling again, he wakes, "Papa,"
I stop, kneel to him.
Gushing out of his dream, he
looks up and points to the trees.

"Were you dreaming?" I ask,
"In the trees, in the trees, up, up, up,"
he delights.

In his eyes, I see the fervent passion of life
awaken. Through his thousand lips, I hear
God.

Paul

Walking early with you
on your birthday,
Orion watching
from the Moon-lit sky.

Cheshire Moon's smile,
knowing you. Father and son
walking but wishing you
were by my side.

Chopping wood,
fixing or riding tractors, red tractors,
and all would be fine,
despite the harshness between us
during childhood years.

My belt pulled tight,
extra hanging and ready
for anything
when I am with you.

You feel close, looking up at you
now, Orion feels closer than 1500
light years, your warrior fills me
with you, time no longer between us.

Martha

You are a Midwest carnival,
pulsing anticipation
of a Saturday afternoon,
blending into evening,
with all the excitement,
all my wanting
to get close enough,
smell your perfume.

Walking around the booths and games,
drinking a soda pop, wanting to win
a giant stuffed teddy bear—for you.

My buddies, classmates,
girls from other schools, neighbors—
all feel the carnival
flirt with their senses.

I imagine you fresh in your tennies.
Then, the fear and pulling back—
what do I say when I'm close enough
to smell your perfume?
The cascading tastes conspire
to serenade your tall body of grace.

You, a dancing carnival,
every step smooth, sure,
with your own expectations,
as we walk to the edge
of the booths and rides.

Behind the trees,
hand in hand, to steal a kiss.
Your warm hands tremble,
hold me tight.
I have waited a year
for this swoon.

Potato Wagon

I hear it again this morning
full of potatoes, rumbling,
bouncing across the wooden bridge.
Tubers tumble, fall,
hit wood planks,
bumping, excited for noise,
thundering across
the heavenly bridge.

In Iowa, stormy skies
are full of danger, excitement,
startling shocks
of lightning, waiting
for thunder to follow.

Wagons filled with locomotive size potatoes
falling, hitting wood,
split wood, break wagons,
test bridges, even the sky falling,
shaking the heavens,
seize a boy's imagination.

My child-mind encompasses
the terrible sound,
making meaning

from a Midwest Bible sky
of sound and light.

Relating these images
to my first grandchild
is exciting.
Telling him how this crack
and flash make sense
to me, afraid in bed
with sky exploding.

Describing to him the awe and wonder
of the family story—
potatoes, wagons, sound, and light.

Anticipating his excitement and surprise,
I tell the story with passion
and purpose, trusting
he will vision and embrace
the mythic story as his own.

After my compelling story,
he turns, looks me in the eye,
and says, "Papa,
that's a bunch of silly talk."

Chandra Again

I touch her shoulder,
asking if the stool next to her
is taken, she turns, says no.
I laugh, recognize her.
Here she is, a year later,
sitting on the same stool.

With a male friend,
possibly a boyfriend, her talk
guarded. She thanks me
for the poem I sent, she says
it touched her, I notice it did.

Between us, she shares as much as she can.
That night like this night,
her eyes a gloss of drink, she talks
of moving to LA as a project manager,
her family still here.

That Thanksgiving eve was
a night remembered for the softness
of skin and hunger for each other.

She leaves with her friend, without
saying goodbye, already too many
questions from him about me.

The world spins,
throwing people together,
apart, together again—each seeking,
not knowing when the spinning will stop.

This Quiet Home

Not waiting for a softer bed,
grandson Jack is napping
on the dining room floor, so quiet
I wonder if he has passed,
but no, he moves.

A fury of action and movement,
now content, asleep with the stars,
his dreamboat afloat on buoyant air,
clouds, thoughts, and me
writing this quiet poem.

Spring flowers blowing through,
smelling sound, blustery coolness washes
the land. I sit with words that incubate
from air, falling, pasting
on a page, waiting for providence.

House so quiet with the young Buddha
sleeping, filling this now holy place
with child-like dreaming. All dreams
of children want to be covered in
peace, happiness, bliss.

His soft silent breath, dreams
escaping on the backs of birds,
carrying messages on the wind.

When he wakes the questions will come.
The fairy tale and myth continuing
the thread of dreams unbroken
since the first man and woman.

Mirroring the Bushmen dreaming
in their sky of stars and lightning,
dream and mystery continue
through his breath on my floor.

This moment,
his path of discovery.

3

Moon and White Buffalo

"Ravens are the birds I'll miss most when I die. If only the darkness into which we must look were composed of the black light of their limber intelligence. If only we did not have to die at all. Instead, become ravens."

-Louise Erdrich

Moon and White Buffalo

White buffalo standing on
high plains plateau searching
herd below for young, old,
bold, infirm, and those buffalo
in the middle, holding both extremes.

Flurry of white snow carefully
settling on white fur, holding
heart's heat. White buffalo sensing
glow of pale full Moon. Scene
of a thousand years roaming;
now, under this white Moon, reflecting
herd's steaming breath.

Heart of white buffalo beating
for all buffalo, knowing Earth
will provide from four directions,
four seasons, four elements,
all abundant in this place,
under quiet Moon.

White buffalo trusting
Moon and Sun roaming,
Father Sky reflecting
solid path of hooves on ground.

Holding of Earth and sky by white
buffalo brings abundance, bridges
seasons, elements, and directions through
time and space, known and unknown.
Vision of white buffalo, animal
and totem rise above the herd, bellows.
Body and breath, choosing this place on Earth
to merge white buffalo with white Moon.

There Will Be Spring

I trust trees more than a newscast,
blog, website. Western
culture doesn't slow
down, no seasons, just more,
more insatiable insecurity.

Last to ripen, first to bud,
the persimmon tree flush of birth.
There will be spring, there will be
another summer, fall, winter;
persimmon says it's so, trusting
trees, signs of nature and growth.

Persimmon taking sun,
warming soil to deepen roots,
buds open when ready, Earth
giving strength to continue the cycle.

Long winter like a hundred years
underground. Taking stock, consolidating,
holding, hibernating within, looking
for self, finding self,
healing green of health.

Flashing a fiery green of flavors,
deep forest green, fresh, electric, yellow green,
leaves smooth, ribbed, mottled, pointed.
All the possibilities now of form,
functioning together, felt as healing.
Renewed by beating rain
drumming to spring's pulse.
Words of healing
speak through lips aflame
with a desire for green again.

Green

Like no other,
persimmon leaves
a luminous, iridescent light.
Sound bursting with a spring smile,
tasting a fresh green,
leaves opening memory
doors of the last fruit.

Growing, rising, belonging
to this day, flushing my eyes
open with envy for this
glorious flutter of green,
sight of gold, frankincense, and myrrh.

A green aroma flowing, padding air.
Day blushing, with a sense
of spring.

Once a year, my garden
window beholds the astonished
sight of a green, like no other.

California Buckeye

On my morning walk,
buckeyes are falling, giving up
homes in branches,
splitting their overcoats.

Buckeyes cautiously emerge,
cinnamon brown balls,
creamy white, round hats,
shy eyes looking skyward.

Are they watching for children to play?
I pick one off the ground, liberating
its overcoat, feel smooth body,
look into round eye, see the world.
I swear it blinks.

The tree next to a road that descends
to the highway where I take a left
on Trenton Road, easy for foot traffic.

I kick one onto the road, it exits
the other side. I aim and want
to kick another so it will roll
to hill's bottom.

I send more on their way, bouncing,
hopping, bumping down the road.

They all veer off.
I choose one with a sharp eye
to stay centered. With soft toe,
I send it on its voyage. Good path,
rolling, bumping,
gyrating, remaining,
picking up speed.

I smile, thinking it will make it.
I see a car coming.

Buckeye rolling down hill,
holding to the middle, at last
moment turns into path
of oncoming car. Right
front tire flattens it.

What are the chances of this
happening in front of my eyes?
Emotions spinning, wondering
flashes. I set this experience in motion.

Others were involved—road,
tree, other road, toe,
breeze, driver, car,
radio song.

Singing,
On the road again…

Broken Bird

This morning,
on my path—
greenish, gray-brown feathers,
ruby red crown,
still warm.

I walked on.

Another messenger
called to higher duty.

Albatross Liberation

The albatross maligned by Coleridge's rhyme
has swallowed a burden in its gut.
Revived for its journey over sea,
has taken the challenge
to clean oceans' plastic.

Surface feeding,
finds multi-colored waste,
looking like food, trusting
ocean to provide.

Albatross skim and scoop,
sight attuned to swimming,
floating forms resting on oceans' table.
They don't understand
dumped pieces tossed
into ocean.

Somehow, they know,
willing to die for us to learn,
willing to atone for the burden
their name implies, wrenching
distress from a human story.

Bringing ingested remnants
back home for their young
to swallow again.

Trust ocean for food, trust
we get the message, release
the burden around our neck.

Flying Circus

Outside my window, a jungle gym,
circus, menagerie of meaning,
for the squirrels. Their playground
includes telephone lines for tightrope
walkers, redwoods for climbing and
jumping, oaks for shade and home,
snacks at fruit trees.

Between death-defying acts,
scurrying through the circuit,
it's all here for squirrels.

Tightrope walking is a breeze,
as they stop mid-span to look and listen
for applause. Ravens responding with
croaking and cawing as squirrels
scurry to redwoods, airborne leaps to
distant branches, flying.

How many thousands of years
did it take squirrel's tiny brain
to develop webbing like wings,
like flying squirrels?

Implanting the thought, the feeling
of soaring into their brains, DNA,
their souls with bird-like curiosity.

Now, each generation continues
this thought, grows webbed skin
to soar like birds, believing.

Happy with circus life,
deciding long ago to explore gravity's
boundaries, soaring, floating,
letting go.

Robin

O, Robin outside my window, plump
as a softball, color of ripening,
finishing the tree's last persimmon.
Pecking each day the sweet,
bright orange flesh.

You sit, wait, contemplate,
turning your head, ruffling feathers.
Not an ounce of doubt in your body,
trusting your song and flight,
belonging.

You perch while I finish my coffee
and now you fly.
I fly too,
surrendering to your flight.

Ancestral rhythm will have you
return, anticipate ripe desire,
sing your beautiful song,
fly your soulful flight.

O, Robin,
this unshaken song, your flight,
does it come simply because
the sun rises on your face?

I Am Stone

I have sparks inside,
sparks from gnashing teeth.
I can be calm and solitary
even while being thrown into a stream.

I don't know what you think of a stone
but I know I came from one.
I descended from a star, rough and jagged,
hot and molten, through an atmosphere
of light, crashing into Earth,
buried until you burst the crust.

Smooth now from centuries
tumbled by water, elements, frozen
and baked, all to harden the exterior,
to keep inner sparks alive.

I have met other rocks and stones.
We gathered, cracked together
making a dragon spewing sparks
of fireflies and stars.

Poetry

Is poetry enough to heal my own mind
from within? This planning, protecting,
scheming, manipulating mind,
constantly seeking safety, keeping out
all intruders as my world gets smaller.

As I let go and allow,
a soft summer breeze
opens the mind to gratitude, becomes
more whole, accepting each moment
as a present, the present.

Each breath a new song,
a new poem, even a new life
with fresh deeper breaths,
more oxygen, more awareness
for the smallest things.

Including bees that make honey
for my steaming cup of tea.
I tell them how happy I am
for this thick, gooey elixir
that brings more than sweetness.

Bees also know of poetry,
their beating wings a rhythm,
a rhyme that sustains poets.

Gratitude sustains the flowers,
enlivens bees,
grows meadows of grace,
keeping bees happy
and honey flowing.

Space—Time

Time and space between raindrops.
Time between tipping your cup
and the warm liquid touching your mouth.

Time between the heron
dropping from its perch and wings catching air.

Time between pressing the pedal
and the vehicle advancing.

Time between out-breath and in-breath,
space and time between footfalls.

Time between flicking a switch and feeling the light.
Time between "ding" and "dong."

Time between crashing wave and hissing retreat.
Time between morning sleep and
the spark of light that awakens conscious thought.

Time between feeling full emotion
and the saline tears forming on your lid.

There is more in-between time than time,
more space that matters.

The Mystery gathers at the edge of thoughts,
and insistently waits for our noticing.

Jackson's Nose

Jackson's nose
smells every green thing,
quivering nostrils,
each vibrates a different tune,
the left side classical,
right side Hip-Hop.

His body sways
to the blue road in between.
He doesn't mind
there's no sound in space.
The smells of chartreuse
enter his nose in octaves,
arpeggios, bumped by clef signs.

Birds add a riff,
black-brown root,
a gong of respect, humming.

He looks at wires in the sky
hears his voice repeated.
Space walking with Bach
worms watch from their squirming trail.

Cacophony laughing
at bent ears of wind

holding the symphony, instruments
of glee. Bees, the back beat
of pollinating stories.

Jackson walks up to me, back-fires
his horn, laying down his track,
sprawling it over tuned keys,
notes of peaches, tuna,
and throaty meow.

Silence goes deep
below the high notes.
He is the bass, below bass,
the purple/black,
below music, below sound.

He flares both nostrils
making music.

Where Are the Bees?

The elephant heart plum,
my favorite, has finished bloom.
Not a honeybee to be seen this spring.
I wonder where and why they have escaped.

Without honey the world will go sour.
Already, the taste of the world is turning
to sourness. The smiles of honey
and laughter, brief.

The bees mirroring a story.
Our ears are stuffed with cotton,
surrounded by loud,
incessant noise and fear.

Bees retreat from the world
going inside, into caves,
and waiting hearts
where they rebuild the sweet
world from the beginning.

They see through many eyes.
Their swarming vision of perspectives
harmonizing a rhythm of
buzzing, fills the air with lifting,
rising, as we hear their verse of
making sweetness.

Jungle Voice

Heard in the sun,
this grunt, this sound from the jungle
was curious, felt like an animal, gnawing.
A log falling while speaking,
a stumbling foot caught in a trap.

At night, this grunt of a smell or thump
became wild—every tree, a message
from the deep amazon jungle
dove into my ears, through heart,
buried into the pit of me.

Later, nightmarish, this voice calling,
asked me to come over the edge
to the deepest afraid parts,
risk a knowing, to be known,
to face the shimmering sound
of awakening.

Vision Wind

Vision Quest, June 2012

O, spirit of the wind,
blow away all my chaff, leave only the seed
of my knowing. Let this seed grow in my heart,
full, open, clear, and strong with possibilities.

O, spirit of the wind,
blow away the critical voices from my speech.
Become the breath for my new voice,
speaking wisdom without right or wrong.

O, spirit of the wind,
blow away the weakness in my legs,
so I can stand strong in the force of adversity
and strengthen my leadership, step by step.

O, spirit of the wind,
blow away the gray clouds in my vision. Allow
me to perceive with the eyes of eagle, to bring
focus and clarity into my thoughts and actions.

O, spirit of the wind,
blow away my separateness from
all things, let me understand the
mystery and the secrets of each day.

4

Bushmen

"The ideal of a single civilization for everyone
implicit in the cult of progress and technique
impoverishes and mutilates us. Every view of the
world that becomes extinct, every culture that
disappears, diminishes a possibility of life."
                                    -Octavio Paz

Bushmen

The Bushmen of the Kalahari Desert
follow lightning. They follow thunder and rain,
mimic electricity, a clicking of words
attracts, connects them with lightning.

The excitement of light in clouds,
special effects quench their thirst.
Lightning and electricity, their gods of survival.

Carrying water in ostrich eggs, they adapt
like walking plants searching for lightning.
Walking, waiting.
Walking, waiting.

Mothers baptize babies to stars and sky,
praying, feeling sacred connection,
announcing each baby blessed
with stardust.

This stone-age tribe, cast aside
by the white man,
the gods of everything.
The white man doesn't depend,
he takes, makes, nothing left to chance.

Bushmen witness food and water
abundance in the Land Rover,
desert ships holding
all they need without a thought
of thanks.

Bushmen see easy abundance
and holes in the bodies of men,
a loss of soul.

Power of authority pressures
Bushmen to fold huts,
live in government housing
away from lightning, stars.

Bless the Bushmen,
who have stories
connecting them forever
to the beginning of time.

Condor, Mountains, and the Girl

A young Quechan girl in the Kinsa Cocha
mountains of Peru notices me hiking alone.
We share water, she drinks lightly,
I gulp. She tells me her name
Flora, delicate new flower,
hearty as the mountain sheep grazing nearby.

Condor, what can you say about
three feathers you dropped for me?
A gift you delivered in bristly air.
A message and blessing I remember
on this day of flying mountains.

Kinsa Cocha, what can you say about
weather echoing
between your peaks? Mists,
marvels of these ancient people
surrounded by your cloak of care.

Flora, what can you say about your soft eyes
looking at me while my heart is breaking
for your blooming smile? You came
curious, and I gave you a coin of
gratitude for gracing my day.

Retirement Tea

I look at your smile, the white
curved smile of my porcelain mug.
First cup of retirement tea, steamy,
smile of my favorite cozy liquid.

Imagine the family
that picked these tea leaves
arriving in my cup.
A family from Sri Lanka, youngest
child daring forth, heroic feet,
her first time to pick tea leaves.

Her small curling fingers pluck
leaves at eye level, coached
by her mothers' deft hands,
she chooses wisely, cautiously,
carefully drops her first leaf
into the basket.

A warm smile explores her face,
an ancient awareness learned
from family. Father and brother
document her signature fingers
etched on leaf, remembering
their own time, beginning.

She squeaks a giggle
as the day begins.

Sitting, pondering tea
and smiling cup, rhyming
the first step of a young girl
in Sri Lanka picking tea leaves,
the brink of imagined gravity
in my new life.

Pandemic Soup Kitchen

Starting my shift, I see homeless
and hungry, waiting, hovering. Abandonment
sticks to the counters,
clings to diffident air.

Day begins with waiting, casual work,
unspools more waiting. Lunch at eleven.
Mostly men, ten at a time,
distancing.

Trays of warm food delivered
to spaces carefully cleaned by volunteers
before the next man sits down.

Each man approaches,
tracking food
that will cure his hunger,
fast.

I watch one man shed
his cap, briefly bow his head.
With a gesture of his finger,
brings a fork of food to touch
his tongue. His question answered,
he begins his ritual.

Men bent from walking
streets and alleys
ask for seconds,
acknowledged with more.
The slow-moving cart
of paper-covered pastries
approaches each man or woman,
they point out their favorite—
some resist.

I pour milk and water. These men
walk on the margins, a razor's edge
of belonging, humbly partaking
of this gift.

Paris

Homage to "January in Paris" by Billy Collins

Thanks, Billy, for writing a poem about Paris
in January, biking, sitting in Parisian cafés.
In my local café I sit looking at stuttering
stop lights, weeds growing through
cracked concrete.

I order my coffee with an extra
dollop of people imagined, speaking French.
But it's nothing like an authentic
French press, or expresso, sitting in Paris.

Coffee in hand, I approach
a tall round table, where you can stand
and drink or sit in a tall chair, but
sitting in this chair requires you
climb a small ladder to seat yourself.

Once seated and elevated I feel
transported to French air space, hearing
the air traffic controller in her marvelous
French accent, clearing me to occupy this seat.

She knew my aircraft number,
"Java three, two, seven, niner, this is Paris control,"

I heard her say, "Cleared for a holding pattern,
at table number ten," her voice magnificent
and caring as I sat thinking of Billy in Paris.
Dreaming of your vision,
I watch people, mostly hustling,
looking busy, not gaily walking,
chatting as the French would.

The French would be intently
exploring each other
with public displays of affection,
called kissing in Paris.
I imagine you watching kissing,
in narrow streets, in parks,
next to statues of Greek gods
and goddesses, in cars stopped briefly
at stoplights, between tall buildings,
and in full view of the *Arc de Triomphe*.

Elevated, and far away, I imagine walking
over a bridge across the Seine. I stop
mid-point, look down over the retro-extinct
railing, at the flowing river of life and
drop a portion of spit over the railing.

Watch it dive for the river, split into
competing blobs and hit the water at the
same time, which would cause a *sacrebleu*
to erupt from the closest Frenchman.

Unacceptable to the French,
we would do this as Midwest kids,
competing for the biggest blob.
The day at my café is not as cold
as your day in January, but I feel
a cold chill thinking of you riding your bike
in the Paris streets, thoughts of poetry,
people, and unfinished poems.

We would compare notes on kissing,
unfinished poems, women in dark rooms,
and spitting over the railing of bridges
spanning the Seine.

I have no rules for the day, only wanting
to feel Paris, as you did, pigeons
occupying every edge of every building;
they watch you watching them.

The last chill I feel was sitting
on my elevated chair imagining myself
in a holding pattern over Paris,
hearing that French voice
of the air traffic controller,
my lips embracing…a cold cup of coffee.

Blowtorch

"I think every woman should have a blowtorch."

-Julia Child

Every female child educated
in the proper use of a blowlamp,
would lessen abuse in the world,
would bring more gender equality.

Girls and women, fitted with twin holsters,
a Bernzomatic for each hand,
in case one runs out of fuel.

There would be quick draw contests,
useful to thwart that touchy neighbor
or family member. A Red Dragon
used to singe an eyebrow
and prevent acts of aggression.

A boon for plastic surgeons,
repairs for grabby hands, hospital
burn units triple staffed, empowered
females snickering about the latest
torching incidents.

Julia was ahead of her time, envisioned
more uses than the harmless *Crème Brûlée*.

Bosses and coworkers would risk getting
their ties singed, and explaining
to their partners.

Torches would be brought into
courtrooms igniting judge's robes
for not abiding a restraining order.

After maiming much of the population,
leaders would learn to work respectfully
with owners of a Spicy Dew Torch.

The use of the blowtorch would return
to more mundane uses—
starting the barbeque grill, lighting
candles for a special dinner,
and the occasional *Crème Brûlée.*

The Potter

Born of minerals,
clay, chemicals, grog, glass, glaze,
fire-sharp, dull, soft, hard, round,
these traits of a potter
tempered by Promethean fire
into a creative body.

Equally, intuitive master of a mystery,
with clay of utility and grace,
sparked by flame.

This Earth beneath your feet,
this constant holding of gravity,
drawing clay and soil into center,
pulling into your center all you need.

Composting, sifting, growing,
harvesting, grinding rock
into a clay of heart, heat, fire.

This clay you came from now in
your hands, to create again
in the crucible of mystery.

Gratitude for the centered
growth in your core,
marvel of a creative life.

This creation crafted, decorated
with flare, care, surrendered to the Muses.
Life-tested and burned by fire, death,
cooled to a form of magic.
Born from this simple clay,
you are made to manifest more life
than you were given, created
with hands centered in trust.

Pond Farm Pottery

"The engaged mind has a watchful heart."

Arriving at the cabin midday,
I unload, put away gear—
never spend the night
on Pond Farm property
in the sheepherder's cabin.

I settle in, hear constant
patter and pelting rain
mixed with sentient voices.

I listen for familiar sounds—
propane truck, visitors, human
and animal. Voices will fade
after a few days of incessant chatter.

They will mix with surroundings,
soak into receptive soil,
bombarding activity between
rain, wind, and sound.

Spinning pottery wheels,
a background for voices speaking
clay and design, asking questions,
random echoes of laughter.

Sun breaks open the room
with new light, nature knocking.
I open the window for fresh smelling
air, hearing the pottery barn.

It stands quietly, breathing,
as I wait for a communal story
told by Marguerite, absorbed,
refreshed season after season.

Pond Farm born fertile
for exploration, creativity.
Voices have subsided, my attention
aroused, the next question
for the pot in front of me,
asking for completion.

I arrive thirsty and curious.
Birds send messages
they may not repeat.

Death Is Not Failure

Every day the death toll is announced,
as though the fallen have failed,
made a mistake,
didn't follow instructions,
took the wrong path home.

They are blamed for going
before their time, unaware
of the covenant with the soul.

Hearing the homeward call
gives respect to the lessons learned,
savors the accomplished artistry.
Every step, act, and decision,
a continual growth for learning.

Each brush stroke reflects
a pallet of colors they chose
to paint their life.

The mood and tone a feast for eyes,
announcing their valiant contribution
as they silently rise.

I Awake on Mars

The burnt orange hue of sky
smells like char of soil,
trees, amber and sage,
air flowing over land
from long ago.

Through windows, I see alien sky,
I sleepwalk through thoughts
of Martian memories,
family, friends, and the time
of the great awakening. Mars,
now slipping beyond safety.

Mistakes of centuries
coming to climax, as the grim reality
of having to leave the doomed planet
will no longer fade
but expose the failed actions
of humans, of circumstances
the result of leaving.

The Martian myth alive in me
has dawned. The stark feeling
of leaving and abandonment
fill my heart with foreboding.

Apprehension of starting over
clashes in crisis with home.

Collision of things and time,
gnashing of people and place,
these memories wake me further,
to sit up in bed, look out and see
I am on Earth.

Land at Pond Farm

This land around Pond Farm,
crafted rain or shine.
Years close to this land, variety
and wildness, oaks, fir, redwood,
madrone, manzanita, and bay,
streams, hills, and mountains.
A feast to hike here alone.

Coming back to the cabin today,
path blocked by flooded stream,
walked across a soaked field,
found a place to cross
with walking stick in the middle
of rushing water. Left the bank
free and vaulted across,
navigating to soggy ground.

Tasting plant-infused air,
each footfall an exploration,
mind at rest, slowing down,
comfortable with now,
step by step.

Days at the cabin are ending.
I have been schooled,
ravished by paintable thoughts,

new mosaics, inner and outer—
writing, walking, listening
to a fresh design.
A span too short
to encompass all, yet
a ravenous craving for more
captures it perfectly.

Each step, glance, view,
thought, an art of opening,
to look deeper, clearer,
more aware, awake.

This month is not dissolving,
but remembering who I am,
and how this place
is a symbol of silent grace.

I said *yes*, to come here,
live here, love here. *Yes*,
brought me to this day—
I say *yes* to tomorrow.

Broken Time

Covid time, the torn fabric of the world,
has thrust upon the small blue-green
planet a free-fall.

Look in the mirror for answers,
not knowing the questions.
Struggle in unaccustomed places,
like this poem searching for ground.

Earth feeling untethered, flying,
floating, circling toward
the unknown, hulking through
the tenuous cosmos.

Yet, we have Earth and soil,
plants that grow, survive, fall to fruition.
The great paradox, quaking our view of
tearing time, asking for something new,
an enduring life of safety.

The tear splitting us will not heal,
a revolutionary rip, sent to our rooms
to look again, respecting
the birthright of belonging.

We are not done,
have not followed through.
There is more healing,
of flesh and bone.
Raise hands to the sky,
lower bodies on bended knee,
toil the heavy Earth.

Begin again, author
an evergreen creation.

Words to Poetry

Without a guide,
words cannot become poetry.
Birds are best, winged messengers
dive, submerge
below famished, ocean forgetfulness.

Choose a "pursuit diver,"
pelican, tern, or booby.
For the deepest dive ask
an Emperor Penguin.

Peck out critical eyes
looking to mask your voice.

Messenger uncovers
buried seeds, wings of imagination
flourish in fertile belonging.

Bridge depths to sky and air,
soar each word
light on thirsty tongue,
voice strengthened, propelled
by phoenix of flames.

Now, words find promised path.
Eyes feel, taste colors,
hear impossible music,
senses become magnets
for magic.
Body explodes, merges,
voices speak passwords
to magnificence.

Fluid pen etching each word
into hieroglyphics, pyrotechnics,
forever, fireworks for the soul.

Brian R. Martens has always been a poet. His first poetry book *Three Raven Gate*, (2019) consists of Haiku and other favorite poems. His podcast is *The Spoken Symbol*. He has a Masters in Organization Development. He offers workshops on Myth/Ancient Stories & Creativity to small businesses and organizations and is a CA Poet In the Schools instructor. He co-hosts the Santa Rosa Arts Center, "Speakeasy" poetry/music/open-mic event. www.brianrmartens.com

Author Statement

I have always been a poet. Images and words are my mentor and guide to my inner life. I write to illuminate, evoke, and transfer my inner gifts and talents to the page which opens myself to guidance and revelation unaffected by the outer world.

I follow the threads of words and symbols that appear and wrangle those thoughts and feelings into a message in a bottle to be found and explored by readers. Patience and structure allow me to form impressions into vivid images on the page.

Writing expresses my love and admiration for the first people, those ancestors that came before, be it animal, human, or plant. I want those voices to speak through me in symbols, rhythms, and revelations. I want my poetry to reveal the deep beauty, tragedy, and unknowable mystery that surrounds me.

This project was made possible, in part, by generous support from the Osage Arts Community.

Osage Arts Community provides temporary time, space and support for the creation of new artistic works in a retreat format, serving creative people of all kinds — visual artists, composers, poets, fiction and nonfiction writers. Located on a 152-acre farm in an isolated rural mountainside setting in Central Missouri and bordered by ¾ of a mile of the Gasconade River, OAC provides residencies to those working alone, as well as welcoming collaborative teams, offering living space and workspace in a country environment to emerging and mid-career artists. For more information, visit us at www.osageac.org

Osage Arts Community